Men of Sturmgeschütz Abteilung 191 pose with their assault gun. After losses during the winter of 1941/42, the unit was sent to Mogilev, Belarus in March 1942 to rest and refit with the new Sturmgeschütz III Ausf.F staying until early June 1942. Given the condition of the vehicle, foliage in the background and the soldier's uniforms, it is a safe assumption that this photograph was taken in the autumn of 1942. Alkett assembled the vehicle between March and early May 1942 and has typical early Ausf.F features: single-piece 50mm armour on the hull and superstructure front, large front mud flaps, a 'Notek' headlamp on the left track guard and armoured headlights on the front tow points. Small arms fire has holed the mudguard and scarred the bow armour.

AMC

Another Ausf.F from StuG.Abt.191, photographed at the same location as the previous page. The new 7·5cm StuK 40 L/43 enabled Sturmgeschütz crews to engage Soviet T-34 and KV tanks at combat distances. Damage to the trackguard and a length of tracks along the side prevent us from seeing any markings. However, the sprayed striped camouflage and sandbags on the front of the superstructure are characteristic features of StuGs from this unit and timeframe.

AMC

An Ausf.F of StuG.Abt.190 in Kerch, Crimea, May 1942. The new 7·5cm StuK 40 gun was capable of knocking out the Soviet T-34 and KV tanks at greater range, unlike previous Sturmgeschütze; interestingly, the gun is not fitted with a muzzle brake. The vehicle, built by Alkett in March-early April 1942, was, along with several other new StuGs, placed at the disposal of the German troops before a major offensive in the Crimea. The 'pot' between the hatches on the roof of the fighting compartment is the ventilator. The engine deck features armoured vent covers over the engine and radiator access hatches and something, possibly concrete, has been added to the top of the protruding sides of the superstructure. In front is its older brother: an Ausf.E.

V.Kozitsyn

3

Another Sturmgeschütz from StuG.Abt.244 near Stalingrad in October 1942. The vehicle is an Ausf.F assembled between June and August 1942, as confirmed by the location of the sectional gun cleaning rods and 'Notek' driving lamp fitted to the track guard. Starting September 1942, this was moved to a central position on the bow armour.

Cegesoma

Above: A good study of an Ausf.F assembled in July or August 1942, with repositioned 'Notek' driving lamp on the bow armour. Having no markings, not even a 'Balkenkreuz', it is impossible to say to whom the vehicle belonged or where the photo was taken.

Right: Infantrymen hitch a ride on the StuG III in the background of the top photo. The commander has his S.F. 14.Z scissors periscope fitted to swivelling its bracket inside his hatch. The spare roadwheel beside the driver's side visor is a field modification. Both photos were taken in the spring or summer of 1943.

2x V.Kozitsyn

This page and opposite: A Sturmgeschütz III Ausf.F on the outskirts of a village in the Rostov steppes, near the River Don in January 1943. The location, style and placement of the tactical number indicate that it belonged to 3./StuG.Abt.201. Between December 1942 and January 1943, the unit was subordinated to the Italian 8th Army and fought in numerous engagements against Soviet armour, losing almost all its assault guns and was subsequently withdrawn from the front. The vehicle was built by Alkett in July or August 1942 and appears to be in good condition except for the 'spiked' gun barrel.

I.Moshchanskij

A wrecked Ausf.F sits on a Kursk street after the liberation of the city. This vehicle belonged to 2. or 3./StuG.Abt.202, who defended Kursk and its suburbs in February 1943. In keeping with the snowy scene, the StuG has been fitted with 'Winterketten', some of which have snapped off their extensions. With additional 30mm armour plates welded to the bow and a single chambered muzzle brake on the 7·5cm Stuk40, it is probable that the StuG was built in June/July 1942. An internal explosion has burst the superstructure apart.

RGAKFD

The same Sturmgeschütz photographed on 9 February and has additional tracks fitted above the driver's position and a spare roadwheel by his side visor. These modifications are characteristic of many Sturmgeschütze from StuG.Abt.202. This view allows us to see that both the engine compartment cover and fighting compartment roof have been blown off. The two houses in the background are 95 and 97 Ulitsa Lenina, both of which still exist at the time of writing.

GAKO

A Sturmgeschütz III Ausf.F from Sturmgeschütz-Brigade.279 near the Church of St. Nicholas in Evpatoria, Crimea in mid-April 1944, which, coincidentally is the same time as the unit transferred all of its assault guns to Sturmgeschütz-Brigade.191, so we cannot be sure exactly which unit left it here. The vehicle has been given a coat of 'Zimmerit' and a set of 'Schürzen'; both of which were added in the field or after refurbishment.

2x GMGOOS

With the Sturmgeschütz increasingly being used in the anti-tank role, it was decided to arm a number with the le.FH.18 10·5cm L/28 gun, the prototype being built on an Ausf.F chassis in September-October 1942. The vehicle was designated Sd.Kfz.142/2 Sturmhaubitze 42 (StuH 42) and only assembled by 'Alkett', of which all but a handful were based on the Sturmgeschütz III Ausf.G. These two are the exception and are part of the 0-serie, from Sturmgeschütz-Abteilung.185, who fought south of Pskov when this photo was taken in early 1943. Both vehicles are on the chassis of late Ausf.F with additional 30mm armour plates welded to the bow. **V.Kozitsyn**

Photos by Russian veteran Aleksey Pamyatnyh, and thanks to his son Aleksey, we have another rare Sturmhaubitze 42 built on the chassis of a Sturmgeschütz III Ausf.F in September/October 1942. The vehicle was destroyed between the villages of Budino, Šastaki and Suchary (roughly 22km east of Mogilev, Belarus) between 21 and 24 June 1944. As a result of Russian tank fire, the ammunition exploded, propelling the superstructure off the chassis. The gun is fitted with an early muzzle brake, the same as field howitzers.

A.Pamyatnyh

Above: The photographer has moved, and we can see more details of the upside-down superstructure. The German national flag with 'Swastika' was probably included for effect and moved from bow armour to gun. Here, a single 'Schürze' remains, indicating that it had been back-fitted with these.

Above right: A rear view, the ground strewn with pieces of the engine compartment and trackguard. Barely visible amidst the wreckage; the tow cable is connected to the tow point, and a faint tactical number ending '3' has been painted between the starter port and 'Balkenkreuz'.

Right: A view of the right side with the remaining 'Schürze'. The object in the background is the base of the gun-mount.

3x A.Pamyatnyh

A column of fresh looking Sturmgschütz III Ausf.F/8s from an unknown unit in an unknown Soviet village in October 1942. The vehicles were assembled in September or October 1942 as the 30mm 'Zusatz Panzerung' is welded to the bow armour - a feature only seen on 'Alkett' vehicles built in September and October. The simplest way to differentiate between the Ausf.F and F/8 is by the towing points: the Ausf.F had bolted-on assemblies, whereas the F/8's were an extension of the hull sides - as seen here. The vehicle in the foreground is one of only a few to be fitted with a ball-shaped, single chamber muzzle brake.
V.Kozitsyn

A side view of one of the Sturmgeschütze from the unit on the previous page, its gun left in the factory heat resistant finish. The photo shows the redesigned rear of the Ausf.F/8 and new air deflectors under the engine air outlet.

F. Freiherr

To Ostketten or not Ostketten? Two Sturmgeschütz III Ausf.F/8s, manufactured in late October - early December 1942, one with one without 'Ostketten'. Markings are a Geschütz number ('5' on the vehicle in the foreground) and a 'Balkenkreuz' on the side. The Abteilung insignia is painted above the driver's side visor, see page 19 for a close up of this. The vehicles belonged to StuG.Abt.232 and were photographed in the Volgograd region of Russia in January 1943.

V.Kozitsyn

Two more Ausf.F/8s from the same unit with Geschütz numbers '1' and '2'. As you might expect, their appearance is similar to the StuGs on the previous page: 'Balkenkreuz' and single-digit Geschütz numbers on radio boxes either side of the fighting compartment, extra tracks on the front of these boxes and the whitewash painted around emblems and markings. The photograph was taken early in 1943.

AMC

An excellent close-up of an Ausf.F/8 from StuG.Abt.232 taken in the spring of 1943. Aside from the retro-fitted loader's MG34 shield, the most significant area of interest are the colour combinations on the vehicle. The StuG was assembled between October and December 1942 by Alkett and should have been delivered in a coat of RAL 7021 'Dunkelgrau', but the significant difference in tone between the gun mantlet and the rest of the vehicle leads us to conclude that the gun and mantlet were painted in RAL 7021 'Dunkelgrau', but the rest of the vehicle was painted RAL 8020'. With the onset of winter, a coat of whitewash was applied which has weathered, making this vehicle an excellent subject for modellers. When applying the whitewash, the crew have taken care not to obscure the 'Balkenkreuz', tactical number and unit insignia on the bow and side armour, and apparently, it was not applied to the front of the mantlet or the gun barrel. No less than ten kill-rings have been painted at the end of the gun barrel. **AMC**

Sturmgeschütz III Ausf.F/8
Sturmgeschütz-Abteilung 232
Russia or Ukraine
Spring 1943

An Ausf.G in the foreground and its predecessor, the Ausf.F, photographed at the beginning of 1943. Both vehicles belonged to StuG.Abt.226, one of the first units to receive the Ausf.G, which started coming off the production lines in December 1942. At the beginning of 1943, this unit was part of the group blocking Leningrad and stationed southeast of the city.

Another early Ausf.G (12.42 - 02.43) from StuG.Abt.226, photographed in the summer of 1943. On the bow armour, between the 'Notek' driving lamp and trackguard, is the tactical number '101'. StuG.Abt.226 started using this placement of the tactical number in 1941. The camouflage pattern appears to be wavy lines over the RAL 8020 basecoat.

V.Kozitsyn

An Ausf.G from 3./StuG.Abt.191 in the Kuban at the beginning of 1943. The photograph clearly shows the new commander's cupola fitted to this model. With seven periscopes and the ability to rotate; the cupola allowed the commander to observe the battlefield while 'buttoned up.' Like Ausf.F/8s assembled after October 1942, this December vintage Ausf.G has 30mm 'Zusatz-Panzerung' bolted to the 50mm armour to the bow.

V.Kozitsyn

A destroyed Ausf.G from SS-StuG.Abt.2 (SS-Panzer.Gren.Div. 'Das Reich') in the outskirts of Kharkov on 16-17 February 1943. The vehicle has been fitted with 'Winterketten', some with 'Mittelstollen' clipped into the centre. Typically these were fitted to every 4th track link for better grip in ice and snow. In comparison to other StuGs in this book, the tracks are fitted backwards. The fighting compartment roof has been blown off the vehicle and now lays on the ground along with an idler wheel. The engine compartment has been blown off too, but that is nowhere to be seen. The tactical marking for the 3.Kompanie of a Sturmgeschütz Abteilung, along with the number '1' have been painted on the trackguard, while a name, possibly 'Bismarck', has been painted above the 'Balkenkreuz' on the side.

GCMSIR

Part of an SS mortar detachment with a Sturmgeschütz III Ausf.G in the Kharkov region, March 1943. The StuG was assembled by Alkett between December 1942 and January 1943 and has a name above the 'Balkenkreuz' and a large stowage bin between the spare roadwheels on the engine deck; both typical of SS-Pz.Gren.Div. 'Das Reich' assault guns in 1943. Some StuGs from this unit had tracks wrapped around the spare roadwheels on the engine compartment.

NARA

Two more early Ausf.Gs (assembled between December 1942 and February 1943) from SS-StuG.Abt.2 in Ukraine in April 1943. The camouflage pattern on the nearest vehicle appears to be wide stripes of RAL 8017 over RAL 7028, and contrary to orders, the wheels have been painted in a similar pattern. The name 'Ziethen' has been applied above the 'Balkenkreuz'.

V.Kozitsyn

A dug-in Ausf.G from 2./StuG.Abt.184. At the end of June 1943, after the refurbishment of forces in Estonia, the unit arrived on the Eastern Front and was stationed in the area of Staraya Russa until October, where the photos on this and the next two pages were taken. Alkett assembled the vehicle in December 1942, and the distinctive steep angle of the superstructure side armour is evident in this photo as is the driver's side visor. The StuG has no camouflage pattern and has been left in its basecoat of RAL 8020, with a layer of concrete on the sloping front superstructure armour. In the background is a Unic Kegresse P107 tractor (Leichter Zugkraftwagen 37). **4x V.Kozitsyn**

Two crewmen with StuGs Ausf.G, and E in the background. The vehicle on the left is the one seen on the previous pages. The photo supports the theory that StuG.Abt.184 tried to increase the protection of their StuGs from late summer/early autumn 1943 with concrete and extra tracks.

V.Kozitsyn

More vehicles from 2./Sturmgeschütz Abteilung 184, shown here on a street in Staraya Russa, October 1943. Thanks to the work of local citizens, it was possible to find an exact location for the photo. It was taken at 6 Voskresenskaya Street, near the junction with Gostinodvorskaya Street, and the building in the right of the photo with its characteristic rounded top facades still exists. Despite the camouflage materials and foliage, some details are visible on the Sturmgeschütz III Ausf.G. The front of the fighting compartment has been covered in concrete like the vehicles on pages 26 - 28, but this vehicle differs by having a loader's MG shield and was probably assembled by Alkett in February 1943.

NAC

The terrible face of war. A knocked out Sturmgeschütz III Ausf.G from StuG.Abt.904 photographed in late December 1943 - early January 1944 near Mazyr, Belarus. Since November, the Abteilung gradually moved from the border towards the city of Mazyr. German forces were eventually forced out of the city on 14 January, and some of the assault guns from StuG.Abt.904 were transferred to the Oktyabrsky area. During February and March, the unit was stationed in the area of Grabov. Next to the dead crewman is a radio-rack; one of three located in the sponsons.

GCMSIR

The same StuG a few days later after much of the detritus has been cleared or looted, and a Nazi flag carefully arranged for the benefit of the camera. The 'Zusatz Panzerung' on the superstructure front and bend in the trackguard above the first return roller indicate that the vehicle was produced by Alkett between February and March 1943. The vehicle belonged to 'A' Batterie.

RGAKFD

An interesting picture from the spring of 1943 with five Sturmgeschütze of four Ausführungs, all from StuG.Abt.202. From left to right: Ausf.E, Ausf.F (with Winterketten on the bow armour), Ausf.C/D, Ausf.F and Ausf.G. The short gunned StuGs have concrete on the sloping front superstructure armour and spare roadwheels on the sides of this. These points, along with significant amounts of extra tracks, are identifying features of Sturmgeschütz III Ausf.C-F/8 from StuG.Abt.202 during 1942 and 1943.   **V.Kozitsyn**

A Nashorn and StuG III really were on thin ice and went through it. The three photographs show the process of recovering the vehicles back to terra-firma using a Sd.Kfz.9 a second Nashorn as an anchor. The StuG, built between March and May 1943, was from StuG. Abteilung.177 or 281 and the Nashorn from s .H.Pz.Jg.Abt.519. The winch of the Sd.Kfz.9 had a direct pull capacity of 7,000kg, but the pulling capacity could be doubled for each snatch block used.

The illustrations below show how this looked on paper and are from 'Merkblatt über die Bergung von Sturmgeschützen' issued by Sturmgeschütz-Schule, Burg in November 1943. Up to three snatch blocks could be used, with a vehicle serving as an anchor, to recover a Sturmgeschütz. This was probably the method used to recover both vehicles in this series of photos.

A. Lyubimov, 2x AMC

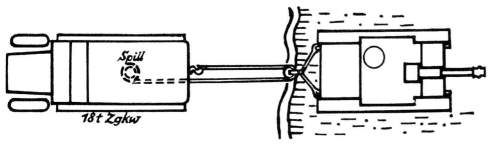

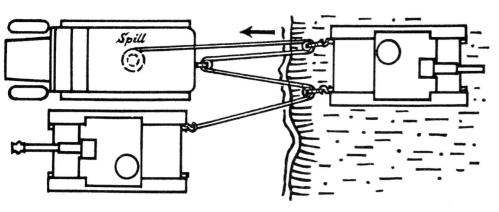

Railcars loaded with the Sturmgeschütze of Panzer-Abteilung 'Feldherrnhalle'. The unit was formed in June 1943 and initially stationed in Southern France before its transfer to Northern France in October. At the end of the year, it was transferred to the Eastern Front. The photo above shows the representative features of StuGs from this unit: spare roadwheels on the front trackguards and engine compartment hatches and stowage bins on the superstructure sides. The freshly painted camouflage pattern has been applied over the spare track, spare roadwheels and hull sides.

J.Haley

More Sturmgeschütze of Panzer-Abteilung 'Feldherrnhalle', these from the 2.Kompanie. All of these vehicles are fitted with 'Schürzen', again with a freshly applied camouflage pattern. In the bottom photo, a Sturmgeschütz is being loaded. Note the wooden 'sticks' inserted into the brackets on the sides of the flatcar; which do not look robust enough to prevent a 24-ton armoured vehicle from slipping off.

3x J.Haley

StuGs from 2.Kompanie drive down a street. The vehicle in the foreground, built by MIAG on Pz.Kpfw.III Ausf.M chassis, has large front mud flaps and additional 30mm plates welded to the bow armour.

J. Haley

The lead vehicle was built by Alkett in late May or early June 1943 on a standard Sturmgeschütz chassis. The second vehicle was assembled by MIAG on a Pz.Kpfw.III Ausf.M chassis. This photo shows the differences between them: mud flaps, bow armour and transmission access hatches.

J. Haley

Men of StuG.Abt.912 pose with one of the Abteilung's Sturmhaubitze 42s. The unit was formed in February 1943 and issued 22 Sturmgeschütz III and 9 Sturmhaubitze in March before being sent to the Leningrad area in April. The Sturmhaubitze shown here was assembled in March 1943. **Inset:** One of the crew poses in the transmission access hatch. The photo shows the vehicle name painted on the welded mantlet and the locking mechanism of the hatch.

2x F.Freiherr

Another Sturmhaubitze 42 from StuG.Abt.912 assembled in March 1943, this time with a weathered coat of whitewash. The gun barrel has burst, leaving it ripped apart and the front of the mantlet gone. The reason for the burst barrel could be a defect in the barrel itself or the 10·5cm round detonating prematurely. Spare tracks are fitted in brackets on the hull and superstructure side - the latter having a black 'Balkenkreuz' painted onto the bracket.

F.Freiherr

Two shots of the same Sturmhaubitze from StuG.Abt.912. It was assembled in March 1943 and differs from the vehicles on the previous pages only with the addition of 30mm 'Zusatz Panzerung' on the bow. It has been given a thorough coating of 'Zimmerit' in the field, which looks more like spattered mud. Like the vehicles on the previous pages, it has extra track in brackets on the hull and superstructure sides, and an indecipherable name painted onto the gun mantlet.

2x F.Freiherr

October 1943; a column in the Kirovograd region headed up by a pair of Sturmgeschütz III Ausf.G from StuG.Abt.261, their unit insignia clearly visible on the bow armour. The nearest vehicle was assembled by MIAG in March/April 1943, the vehicle behind by MIAG or Alket between May and September. **Cegesoma**

An excellent study of a Sturmgeschütz named 'Eloson' from StuG.Abt.190 in 1943. The vehicle was built by MIAG between March and early April and sent to the unit as a replacement. The armour plate in front of the driver no longer has holes drilled for KFF.2 periscope; moreover, the plate is an early version with four rather than five bolts above the driver's visor. The leading edges of the 'Schürzen' are unusual as they have been reinforced with 'L' section steel. The unit insignia tactical marking for a Sturmgeschütz-Abteilung is painted clearly on the nose.

2x AMC

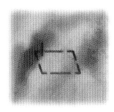

The photos on this and the next page show Sturmgeschütz Abteilung 189 south of Orel in May or June 1943.

Above left and right: A StuG III Ausf.G, built by Alkett in February or March 1943, overcomes the obstacle. StuG.Abt.189 used a system of letters to identify vehicles in their batteries. This one has the letter 'H' on the side of the superstructure and starter crank cover. The letters and tactical markings have been underlined - a feature of StuGs from this unit in 1942/43, and could also be painted in black. Another unique feature is the style of 'Balkenkreuz', with a thin black outline. The vehicle has a rail around the engine deck made of flat metal strips - a field modification which would become a factory fitment later in the war.

Bottom: Another StuG navigates the same obstacle, this one with the letter 'G' on the starter crank cover. This vehicle is similar to the 'H' vehicle with a railing around the engine deck, tracks on the sides of the fighting compartment and 'Balkenkreuz' with a black outline. The camouflage pattern consists of stripes of varying widths.

3x WDR Digit

Top left: This Sturmgeschütz III Ausf.G has a machine gun shield on the fighting compartment roof, but it still has two holes for the driver's periscope. A barely visible letter 'A' has been painted at the front of the side armour.

Top right: This StuG has 'Schürzen' and was assembled between late March and May 1943. Its identifying letter 'J' is painted onto a dark rectangle and underlined. Note how the construction of its engine deck railing differs slightly from the other vehicles. The vertical supports are made of angle iron, and the length of rail is much longer, almost reaching the fighting compartment.

Bottom: The 'Schürzen' on this vehicle have been spray-painted in wide stripes. Like the vehicle above, it has long engine deck railings and only has the identifying letter 'C' on the side, not on the rear. The three logs fixed to the 'Schürzen' mounts and rear plate is a feature often seen on StuGs of StuG.Abt.185 and 189 in the summer of 1943.

3x WDR Digit

Two dead crewmen from StuG.Abt.244 lie next to their Sturmgeschütz after being knocked out in the Orel region of Russia in July 1943. This unit was reorganised in March after its destruction at the beginning of 1943 in the Stalingrad pocket. It returned to the Eastern Front in June and took part in Operation Citadel where it suffered significant losses. Details such as the method of stowing extra tracks on the engine deck, vertically mounted spare roadwheels either side of the engine compartment and small rectangular strips of steel as retainers for the 'Schürzen' are all particular to StuG.Abt.244. The rear plate has a 2 or 3 digit tactical number and the unit insignia. **RGAKFD**

August 1943, Soviet tankers study a Sturmgeschütz III Ausf.G captured during the 'Belgorod-Kharkov' offensive. It has the temporary insignia of 11.Panzer-Division on the bow near the left track, although at this point, the unit did not have assault guns but had StuG.Abt.911 attached. The rail around the engine deck and bracket welded to the sides of the fighting compartment are field mods.

RGAKFD via I.Moshchanskij

Above and pages 50 and 51: A walkaround of a Sturmgeschütz manufactured in March/April 1943 and knocked out in the Orel area a few months later, in July or August. The vehicle, from StuG.Abt.185, has come under artillery or air attack as there is a crater, and shrapnel marks on the superstructure and commander's cupola. The two holes in the remaining 'Schürze' do not appear to correspond with damage on the vehicle. The placement of the tactical number '28' next to the driver is a distinguishing feature of StuGs from this unit in 1943.

The rear of the vehicle from the previous page. Some field modifications are visible here, such as the hand/foothold welded to the rear plate under the tactical number and the location of the jack at the back of the engine deck - usually found near the engine air intake on the right trackguard. The 'spikes' sticking out of the spare roadwheels on the engine deck are track pins.

RGAKFD

The right side gives a good idea as to the camouflage pattern employed by StuG. Abt.185 in 1943: blotches and stripes over the basecoat of RAL 7028 'Dunkelgelb'. An explosion next to the track tore some of the rubber from the first roadwheel, return roller and damaged the trackguard. On the roof, the loader's hatches have been blown off, indicating an internal explosion.

RGAKFD

Sevastopol became one of the last German strongholds in the Crimea. Some personnel of 17.Armee managed to escape through the city, leaving nearly all of their armoured vehicles and heavy weapons, including a number of assault guns, such as this seemingly intact Sturmgeschütz.

L.Archer

Soviet officers pose with another Sturmgeschütz, assembled in September or October 1943, and a partially dismantled Sd.Kfz.10/5 in the same area in May 1944. Both assault guns on this page have a non-standard 'Zimmerit' pattern and have no camouflage, so probably belong to the same unit.

I.Moshchanskij

Soviet troops look over an abandoned StuG III Ausf.G near Sevastopol in May 1944. The vehicle, assembled between March and May 1943 by Alkett, is missing a roadwheel on the far side. The field-applied 'Zimmerit' pattern is similar to the vehicle on page 10, which also has no camouflage pattern either. The vehicle belonged to StuG.Brig.279 until StuG.Brig.191 took over their vehicles in April 1944.

A collection point for German vehicles in Sevastopol. Among them is the StuG from the previous page with its missing second roadwheel. This elevated view allows us to see the 'Zimmerit' on the vents on the engine access hatches. **Opposite:** German and Romanian prisoners are paraded past the camera, just a few of the thousands captured here. More or less every vehicle, except the two Hummels have been left in their basecoat of RAL 7028 'Dunkelgelb'. The Sturmgeschütz in the foreground, built by Alkett in March-early June 1943, stands out among the StuGs as it has spare tracks and tool holders on the sloped front superstructure armour of the superstructure.

A.Haldej, V.Kulikov

Another collection point for German vehicles and weapons in the Sevastopol area. The Sturmgeschütz III Ausf.F has a rail around the engine deck and bolted-on 30mm 'Zusatz Panzerung'; features not often seen on these vehicles. To its left is an Ausf.G with cast mantlet, an Ausf.F and three Ausf.Gs with welded mantlets. Last in line is an Sd.Kfz.131 'Marder II'.

A wider, slightly better view showing how the two Ausf.Fs differ in their method of fixing the 'Zusatz Panzerung' to the bow armour. Further down the line, one of the welded mantlet Ausf.Gs is missing the front of the mantlet; this is the vehicle shown at the bottom of page 52. The 2cm Flak 38 in the foreground has a large number of kill markings on the gun shield.

I.Moshchanskij

Even though they have the same 7·5cm StuK 40 L/48, the gun barrel of the cast mantlet Sturmgeschütz appears shorter than the welded mantlet vehicles due to the mantlet being longer. The combination of this mantlet, 'Zimmerit' and 360° rotating commander's cupola means that it was manufactured in November 1943 by Alkett. Note that both Ausf.Fs have concrete applied to the sloping armour above the driver and 'Zimmerit' on the gun mantlet.

I.Moshchanskij

Russian soldiers walk past a destroyed Ausf.G built by Alkett in the spring of 1943 and photographed near Sevastopol station in May 1944. Crew demolition or the ammunition exploding is the likely cause of this much destruction. The metal cylinders either side of the engine deck are 'Filzbalg' air pre-cleaners.

L.Archer

Another Sturmgeschütz knocked out in the vicinity of Sevastopol. It was built by MIAG between November 1943 and January 1944. At first sight, it looks unusual with all-metal return rollers, a deflector in front of the commander's cupola and without 'Zimmerit', which was introduced before the introduction of these components. However, this is not so as 'Zimmerit' is present but the quality of the photograph makes it difficult to distinguish. **GMGOOS**

An interesting pair of Sturmgeschütz III Ausf.G from StuG-Brig.277 photographed between Vilnius and Kaunas, Lithuania in early July 1944. Both StuGs were assembled in March/April 1943, but have an unusual combination of features: 30mm 'Zusatz Panzerung' on the bow, cast gun mantlet and 'swinging' 'Schürzen'. The longer these vehicles spent in combat, the more parts were replaced and fixed, leading to hybrids as we see here. The Sd.Kfz.3 'Maultier', in the left the photo was one of 9 allocated to a Sturmgeschütz Brigade for ammunition transport.

V.Kozitsyn

Summer 1943. Soviet soldiers examine an abandoned Sturmgeschütz III Ausf.G from an unknown unit in the Oryol or Bryansk region. Possible owners are StuG.Abt.189, 190 or 909. Note the compacted dirt on the roadwheels - it is possible that it was recovered without its tracks.

GCMSIR

Men of the Bryansk Front examine an abandoned StuH 42 from 1./StuG.Abt.190. The photo was taken in the area of the Kaluga, Bryansk or Orel regions of Russia in August 1943. The towing clevises in the tow points and the absence of visible damage, other than missing periscopes from the commander's cupola, suggest that it may have broken down. The vehicle was assembled between mid-May and June 1943.

GCMSIR

This page and opposite: An excellent comparison of new Sturmhaubitze 42 (this page) and Sturmgeschütz III Ausf.G. Both were assembled by Alkett in August 1943 and issued to StuG.Abt.261 at Altengrabov, where these photos were taken, before the unit was sent to the Eastern Front in the September. The vehicles have various markings chalked onto the front, the most notable of which is the 'lightning' marking - meaning unknown

2x V.Kozitsyn

A totally destroyed Sturmgeschütz III Ausf.G from 2. or 3./Pz.Abt.FHH of Panzergrenadier-Division 'Feldherrnhalle' in the village of Kisel'ki, 16 km east of Mogilev in Belarus. The StuG, assembled by Alkett between May and October 1943, was destroyed by a direct hit by a FAB-100 bomb during a Soviet airstrike on 24 June, blowing off the roof of the fighting compartment and engine cover. There are also two scars from armour piercing shells on the front of the vehicle. It is notable that, despite the level of destruction, there are no signs of fire and the rubber tyres are still on the roadwheels.

2x TsAMO

Sturmgeschütz crews could be inventive with their methods of increasing protection, but this Sturmhaubitze 42 from StuG.Brig.210 is particularly interesting. In addition to the oft-seen concrete and extra tracks, a large metal sheet has been bent over the bow armour and secured at the bottom with metal straps. We do not know if it was intended as spaced armour or if there was anything behind it, but the small square-shaped hole indicates that it probably started life as a section of 'Schürze'. As with most other assault guns of StuG.Brig.210, the vehicle has concrete over the front of the fighting compartment and extra tracks there too - in this case from a Russian KV-I. The tracks carried on the side are 'Winterketten'. Lastly, an old wound has been patched on the side of the gun mantlet.

F.Freiherr

The photos on the next three pages were taken by a soldier in 8th Guards Zaporozhye Separate Reconnaissance Artillery Battalion approximately 50 km north of Nikopol and 50 km east of Krivoi Rog, Ukraine in January and February 1944. The image above was taken between the villages of Nikolaevka and Miropol in January and shows a Sturmgeschütz assembled between the end of May and September 1943 which may have been from StuG.Abt.232, 236 or Pz.Jg.Abt.228 of 16.Panzergrenadier-Division. An internal explosion has blown off the roof, the front of the gun mantlet and the engine cover - possibly as a result of the crew setting demolition charges in the fighting and engine compartments. The front elements of the running gear have disappeared too: drive sprocket, some roadwheels and leading return roller.

V.Kozitsyn

On the southern outskirts of Nikolaevka, 50 km north of Nikopol on 14 January 1944; an Alkett StuG assembled between May and October 1943 and from StuG.Abt.232, 236 or Pz.Jg.Abt.228. It was destroyed in a German counterattack and knocked out on 10 January, but not before a firefight, judging by the empty shell casings around the vehicle. The engine compartment seems to have suffered the most damage as the access hatches have been blown open, buckling some and blowing off their ventilation covers. A couple of interesting details emerge upon closer inspection such as a handle on the opened transmission access hatch and metal strips attached to the trackguard to hold the front and rear 'Schürzen' in place.

V.Kozitsyn

Another StuG sacrificed to Soviet gunners. The same vintage and from the same unit as the previous page, this one was photographed on 3 February near Sorochino, 6 km southwest of Nikolaevka, after being knocked out two days earlier. The two well-defined holes in the rear 'Schürze' were probably made by 76·2cm armour-piercing rounds, which could easily penetrate the 30mm side armour of a Sturmgeschütz. The rear 'Schürze' has a steel strap securing it to the trackguard.

V.Kozitsyn

Losses for Heeres-Sturmartillerie-Brigade 191 in the area of Belgrade, Yugoslavia, September 1944. The two Ausf.Gs in the foreground were built by MIAG. The lead vehicle has a hole in the driver's side of the superstructure and is missing the first return roller. It was manufactured in the spring or summer of 1943. This StuG and StuH 42 in the background have a similar camouflage pattern, unlike the smoking StuG which is only painted in RAL 7028 Dunkelgelb.

A.Haldej

This photo shows the debris left on the engine deck, and it is highly likely that the vehicles were pillaged for useful items, hence the opened stowage bins. It is also quite likely that the smoke coming from the Sturmgeschütz is not from combat, but was staged for the photo as this was a common occurrence across all armies.

A.Haldej

The smoking StuG was built on a Pz.Kpfw.III chassis. The 30mm plate welded to the 50mm bow is a feature of MIAG built Sturmgeschütze manufactured between February and December 1943. Here we can clearly see the single-door transmission hatches and a coil of extra tracks. In the background are a wrecked truck and trailer. **A.Haldej**

The other side of the Sturmhaubitze 42 from the previous pages showing the roof of the fighting compartment with its circular fitting for a 'Rundumfeuer-MG' mount. Due to problems with the supply, manufacturers did not start fitting this equipment until July 1944, and not on all vehicles. It would take until October for supplies to be sufficient enough to equip all vehicles leaving the factories.

A.Haldej

The Sturmhaubitze from the previous pages was photographed on 5 January 1945 by a Bulgarian military photographer at a display of captured German equipment in Belgrade. It is remarkably complete with only some items from the engine deck and a pair of 'Schürzen' missing. The lack of a shot deflector in front of the commander's cupola is an unusual sight for a vehicle with 80mm frontal armour and coaxial MG.

2x MPAB via L.Archer

Sturmgeschütz '312' from StuG-Brigade.244 was attacked by Soviet aircraft on 23 June 1944 while crossing the bridge over the river Basya at Chiĺkaviči - about 30 km northeast of Mogilev. The bridge was completely destroyed, but the StuG suffered no serious damage. The assembly plants installed a shot deflector in front of the commander's cupola from Autumn 1943, but the crew have taken this a step further by covering the area to the left of the cupola with concrete. For even more protection they have added generous amounts of spare tracks.

BGAKFFD via L.Archer, TsAMO

Men of 1./StuG.Brig.322 with a damaged Sturmgeschütz near Ostrowiec Świętokrzyski, Poland in the Autumn of 1944. The vehicle, assembled by MIAG between November 1943 and April 1944, ran over a mine, wrecking the drive sprocket, front shock absorber and first roadwheel. We probably see the vehicle partway through repair because two of the other roadwheels have been removed as has a suspension swing-arm. The loader's MG34 is in the air defence position atop its armoured shield. **V.Kozitsyn**

Another Sturmhaubitze from 1./ StuG.Brig.322, graphically showing how ineffective concrete was at keeping armour piercing rounds from penetrating a vehicle's armour. The AP round penetrated the top of the superstructure directly in the path of the commander, who was killed in this instance. The injured gunner can be seen in the commander's cupola. Extra tracks have been 'concreted-in' to the front of the superstructure, in the left of the photo.

V.Kozitsyn

Red Army soldiers examine a Sturmgeschütz from SS-StuG.Abt.11 of 11.SS-Frewilligen-Panzergrenadier-Division on the outskirts of Kipen (12 km southwest of Krasnoe), Russia on 20 January 1944 after the town fell the day before. The StuG was assembled by Alkett in late November - December 1943 and has 'Zimmerit' and the new cast mantlet, introduced in early December. Close inspection of the mantlet shows mouth and eyes had been painted on; a feature of StuGs from this unit. It is not known if the StuG was destroyed or abandoned but there is some damage to the second and third roadwheels.

2x CGAKFFD

An 'incident' involving a StuG from StuG-Brigade 912 somewhere on the Eastern Front in 1944. The short metal bars welded to the sloping plates on either side of the gun were to hang extra tracks in an attempt to increase protection. The 'Schürzen' on the far side have been removed and now lay on the ground.

F.Freiherr

Red Army soldiers look over knocked out and abandoned German vehicles in the Minsk area, July 1944. The Pz.Kpfw.IV Ausf.H, tactical number '223' has been pushed off the road and the Sturmhaubitze 42 is probably next in line for removal. The vehicle, built between the end of April and May 1943, has a layer of concrete around the outside part of the commander's cupola; a field modification. The location and features indicate that this StuH 42 was from Sturmgeschütz Brigade 244. The hole in the mantlet predates factory preparation for a coaxial machinegun (August 1944) and is possibly a field mod to incorporate this. Note that one set of its tracks are on backwards. **V.Kulikov**

A Sturmgeschütz from StuG.Brig.232 destroyed in the area of Raseiniai, Lithuania in August/September 1944. The superstructure and hull sides have the recognisable checkered MIAG 'Zimmerit' pattern. It has virtually nothing left that would identify when it was assembled, apart from the tracks having a groove in the top of the track-horn, which was introduced mid-1944. This is not sufficient for a positive identification.

TsAMO

Also in the area of Raseiniai is this pile of scrap, also from StuG-Brigade 232. It features all-metal return rollers, 80mm bow armour and the gun mantlet (welded like most MIAG vehicles) is drilled for a coaxial machine gun. Note the absence of 'Zimmerit' on the bow armour. Both this and the previous StuG were destroyed by Soviet ground attack aircraft.

TsAMO

Another view of the StuG from the bottom of the opposite page, revealing a few more details and its catastrophic damage. The combination of a hole for a coaxial MG in the mantlet, 80mm bow armour and gun travel lock indicates that it was assembled by MIAG in early July 1944.

E. Barkova

Russian soldiers look over a destroyed StuG southwest of Laura (now called Lavry), a village 26 km southwest of Izborsk, Russia. Between 3 and 5 August 1944, Soviet forces bypassed the village to the south with aggressive attacks, blocking the roads in and out of the village. This StuG was hit during one of the German counterattacks on 3 and 4 August and belonged to StuG-Brigade 261, whose insignia is visible on the bow armour near the right track. The vehicle was assembled by MIAG in the spring of 1944 and has the name 'Bonte' painted onto the mantlet.

TsAMO

This view shows the level of destruction suffered by the Sturmgeschütz. The engine compartment has been completely destroyed and the fighting compartment roof is nowhere to be seen. A return roller, complete with its mount, lies next to the Russian soldier. **TsAMO**

A trophy for Soviet tankers on the edge of a wooded area northwest of Lavry. Soviet forces blocked the main northwesterly route from Lavry (then known as Laura) at 21:00 on 5 August, forcing the German defenders to withdraw leaving this StuH, from StuG-Brigade 261, behind. Its far track is broken - perhaps this is why it was abandoned? It was assembled by Alkett, as all Sturmhaubitze were, between March and May 1944 and features a welded gun mantlet and all-metal return rollers. Markings are the same as the StuG on the previous page: brigade insignia and tactical sign for a Sturmgeschütz unit on the bow and an unreadable name on the gun mantlet. **TsAMO**

This StuG was knocked out by a Russian anti-tank gun about 3 km north of Wołomin, Poland at the end of August 1944 and photographed on 1 September. The vehicle, possibly from 3.SS-Panzer-Division, was assembled in June or early July 1944 by MIAG, the three 'Pilze' mounts on the roof and lack of gun travel lock helping to date it. The left side has three clear penetrations from Russian armour-piercing rounds; above the driver, on the superstructure side and next to the second return roller. The ensuing explosion has flipped the roof so we can see that both the 'Nahverteidigungswaffe' and 'Rundumfeuer' MG openings have been closed off.

2x TsAMO

This photo shows men of an unknown unit on the Eastern Front spraying a camouflage pattern onto the roof of a Sturmgeschütz III Ausf.G, with the first line sprayed in front of the commander's cupola. The vehicle was built by Alkett between June and September 1944 and has a late pattern roof with 3 'Pilze' mounts for a crane and fittings for a 'Rundumfeuer' MG.

V.Kozitsyn

Later in the painting process, and the StuG now sports a striped camouflage pattern, including on the inner face of the 'Schürzen'. In the background is a turretless Russian KV tank. During 1943, some captured KV tanks were sent back to the Army Group to be used as recovery vehicles. **V.Kozitsyn**

Page 92 and left: A Sturmhaubitze 42 from Sturmgeschütz-Brigade 249 in Ukraine, April-May 1944. It has been fitted with 'Ostketten' and a muzzle brake from 10·5cm leFH 18M with its distinctive baffles, while the single-piece 80mm armour plate to the right of the gun indicates that the vehicle was manufactured in April 1944. Armour has been reinforced with concrete and both German and Russian tracks. A three-digit tactical number ending in '2' has been painted onto the 'Schürzen'. In July, the unit was encircled near the town of Brody, Ukraine and lost all its heavy equipment.

Above: Another of Sturmgeschütz-Brigade 249's AFVs, this a Sturmgeschütz. It was manufactured much earlier than the StuH - between March and early May 1943 - but has all the distinguishing features of the unit: T-34 tracks fixed to the bow, German tracks fixed to the fighting compartment and concrete reinforcement of the front sloping armour.

3x AMC

'Irma', a StuG from Sturmgeschütz-Brigade 249, was lost during the attempted breakout near Brody, Ukraine between 17 and 21 July 1944, during which the Brigade lost all of its heavy equipment. The vehicle was not knocked out, but stuck in the mud and abandoned. It was assembled by MIAG between March and June 1943, the telltale sign being the transmission access hatches only have a locking mechanism on the right hatch. After a year in combat, the vehicle has undergone several modifications, a unique one being the additional 30mm armour plate on the bow, which is taller than usual and possibly the result of a repair.

RGAKFD

Pages 96-98: An interesting, if poor quality, set of photos taken by a Soviet artillery brigade on their way to the Frisches Haff in March 1945. Potential German units were the Fallschirm-Sturmgeschütz-Abteilung from Fallschirm-Panzergrenadier-Division 2 'Hermann Göring', Sturmgeschütz-Abteilung 1240 of 170.Infanterie-Division, StuG-Brigades 259 or 279. The two StuGs on this page were knocked out northeast of Wesselshöfen, a village that no longer exists, the nearest places being Il'ichevka and Novoselovo in Kaliningrad.

Top: An Alkett built vehicle in a defensive position with a 7·5cm Pak 40. **Bottom:** In the same wooded copse is this StuG, completely destroyed by Soviet artillery. Note how the gun mantlet has slid down the gun barrel.

2x TsAMO

This StuG has become stuck near Grünwiese, another village that no longer exists, the nearest villages being Il'ichevka and Bol'shedorozhnoye in Kaliningrad. Assembled by Alkett between October 1944 and January 1945, it has ice sprags in the tracks and the remains of a winter camouflage. The 'Schürzen' are interesting as they are pivoted from the trackguards - although only one remains, it allows us to see how they were mounted. The upper 'Schürzen' on the superstructure sides were fixed.

TsAMO

Another StuG from the same unit. Despite the similarity between the two, they are different vehicles photographed in different places. A MIAG vehicle assembled after September 1944, it was abandoned southeast of Laukitten, now Bol'shedorozhnoye in Kaliningrad. The method of fixing the 'Schürzen' is roughly the same as the vehicle above and differs only in some details. The upper 'Schürze' closely resembles the shape of the superstructure sides. The rear return roller has been replaced in the field.

TsAMO

Two wrecks at Fedderau,1 km northeast of Primorskoye. The vehicle on the right has a combination of loader's MG shield and single-piece 80mm armour in the superstructure front, an unusual combination that dates it to April or May 1944.

TsAMO

Another victim of Soviet artillery, this time near Wolittnick (now Primorskoye, Kaliningrad), on the Heiligenbeil to Ludwigsort railway line. The vehicle is similar to those on page 96, and was positioned by a revetment for the anti-tank role.

TsAMO

A Sturmgeschütz, built by Alkett between January and May 1944, and a Jagdpanzer 38, destroyed in the vicinity of Partheinen (now Moskovskoye), 2km south-west of Primorskoye.

TsAMO

Pages 99-102: For Sturmhaubitze '2331', the war ended in a bomb crater on the outskirts of Königsberg in April 1945. The vehicle has a hull dating from May 1943 with bolted-on 'Zusatz Panzerung' on the bow and a superstructure from June-July 1944 with fittings for a 'Rundumfeuer-MG' mount and three 'Pilze' mounts in the roof. The superstructure was probably a replacement for a damaged one. The 'Nahverteigungswaffe' opening in front of the 'Rundumfeuer-MG' mount has been closed from the inside; typical of Alkett vehicles. MIAG StuGs had a round metal plate bolted to the outside.

I.Moshchanskij

The back end of the Sturmhaubitze showing details particular to vehicles manufactured in 1943: four rows of three conical bolts on the rear wall and the dome-shaped access port at the bottom of the hull.

A row of four Sturmgeschütze destroyed by Soviet ground-attack aircraft on the 1st Ukrainian Front area of operations in April 1945. The vehicles are all from the same unit, but we cannot confirm which. The large German applied Swastikas and style of tactical numbers are similar to that of Kampfgruppe Ritter, but this is pure conjecture. We will look at each in more detail on the following pages.

TsAMO

First, as the photographer moved up the line is StuG '132', which was assembled by Alkett after September 1944 and featuring a unique pattern of 'Schürzen'. The roof has been blown off the fighting compartment and the engine deck has shifted. Its camouflage pattern is interesting too with a combination of styles on the skirts and vehicle armour. The Germans painted the 'Swastika' and tactical number, but the БА-919 marking is Russian.

TsAMO

Moving up the line is '134', whose style of tactical number differs from '132'. At first glance, its 'Schürzen' appear to be standard issue, but they are lower in height and the two spare roadwheels, normally fitted to the radiator covers, have been relocated to the rear of the vehicle. An explosion has blown the roof off the fighting compartment. The front 'Schürzen' panel gives an idea as to how the camouflage pattern would have looked before the StuG was knocked out.

TsAMO

StuG '113' seems to have suffered the least damage of the four vehicles and was assembled after September 1944 by Alkett. The style of tactical number differs from the others and has a thin dark border.

TsAMO

Right: At the head of the column is '136', whose unusual 'Schürzen' are of the same pattern as '132'. An explosion in the engine bay has pushed the heavy engine compartment cover almost off the back end; the force of the explosion taking the engine access hatches clean off. The ensuing fire has then spread to the last two roadwheels.

TsAMO

Below: Two more StuGs from the same unit and area in April 1945. Vehicle '124' was assembled after September 1944 and it appears that only the gun barrel has been damaged - in this case, demolished by the crew, so possibly the vehicle broke down or ran out of fuel.

2x TsAMO

StuG '151' or '15' was an Alkett vehicle and once again, its roof has been blown off. The only remaining 'Schürzen' are those between the roadwheels and return rollers; those on the side of the superstructure have come away, revealing a length of six Panther tracks.

TsAMO

Soviet soldiers inspect German wreckage in East Prussia, April 1945. The MIAG Sturmgeschütz in the foreground was manufactured between May and early September 1944 and has a hole for a coaxial MG, which MIAG introduced in May. The two metal strips directly in front of the driver's vision block appear to be a vane sight, used to roughly point the vehicle on target, after that the gunner could make the final adjustments. This was more usually seen in front of the commander's hatch or cupola on gun tanks. The vehicle was destroyed by an internal explosion which unseated the roof.

GCMSIR

The photos on pages 110 - 112 were taken by Vasily Guzikov while serving in Hungary in 1945; this Sturmgeschütz captured south of Székesfehérvár. The 4-digit tactical number on the 'Schürzen' leaves no doubt that the vehicle was from 1./H.Sturm.Art.Brig.303. Sturmgeschütze from this unit had the number '3' in front of the standard 3-digit tactical number. Model makers take note of the whitewash and how it was not worked into recesses or under the gun mantlet. The 'Schürzen' have scratches in the paintwork too, from travelling through close-country. The vehicle was produced by 'MIAG' in December 1944.

I.Guzikov

The business end of StuG '3134', which, on the face of things, looks intact. Closer inspection shows that an armour-piercing round has hit the bow armour and taken off the tow point. It would seem likely that this has damaged the final drive and disabled the vehicle. A couple of interesting details are evident here; the roadwheel fixed to the side of the superstructure, which incidentally can be seen on another Heeres.Sturm.Art. Brig.303 vehicle on page 112, and that the leading 'Schürze' has been whitewashed on its inside face. The unit received a large number of new StuGs in January 1945.

I.Guzikov

Above left and above: No prizes for photographic quality. More images from Vasily Guzikov. Radio-men look over and pose with a destroyed StuG in the area of Lake Velence, Hungary in February or March 1945. The roof of the fighting compartment has been blown off, and the tracks are gone. Although the photos are poor quality, we can see a hole in the side of the superstructure. MIAG assembled the vehicle in December 1944, and like the vehicle on the preceding pages, it was issued to H.Sturm.Art.Brig.303.

Left: March 1945, Lake Velence once again. A whitewashed Sturmgeschütz from an unknown unit has ended its war in a bomb crater or ditch. Despite the poor quality, an Alkett 'Zimmerit' pattern is visible on the superstructure side. Or is it a mark in the photo?
3x I.Guzikov